The Surgeon

in the name of Jesus. Love

Linnea Quyen

ty to use, or

ency of the

ʒ Platform

Dedication

This is all to Jesus, for mending my heart ❤

Preface

Herein lies accounts of Jesus, the Father's Love for us and a touch of Heaven through a mix of actual events, fictional storytelling, personal happenstance, and spiritual exchanges and visions.

Acknowledgements

Thank you to each one of you for believing in and
continuing to support me:

• my daughter, husband, siblings, parents, in-loves and
close friends for taking me just as I am and loving every
part of me.

• my therapists for openly and kindly listening to me,
and compassionately guiding me in unlocking my past
inner child-trauma wounds and regaining my voice and
sense of self.

• those who I have met and befriended through multiple
churches and worship + choir over the past three years
— without you, I would not have grown more deeply in
relationship with God, fellowshipping with other
believers in Christ, understanding even more tangibly
what His Love in full could be, or my love for
music/worship and the power it has to connect us
together and speak to + in us.
• complete strangers and those who follow me online.

It has meant the world. Thank you ❤
From the bottom of my heart.

And lastly, but most importantly, thank You God, for another privilege to share how you have been working in and through my life.

Without You, I would be nothing.

1. The Jade Colored Bench

She was a young girl, praised for her silence and ability to follow directions. This was how she believed she was good and lovable. She was disciplined, made to feel shamed, bad about herself otherwise. Through these, she adopted a way of being that was quiet and as unseeable as possible, so as not to draw any attention to herself.

Yet, as she grew older, differing and internally conflicting directions came her way. When she was told to "speak up" in class by teachers, she became uncomfortable and embarrassed, at times stumbling over words but continuing on anyway. Pink, flushed in the cheeks. Sweaty in the palms.

Expressing opinions or ideas for topics of discussion in any situation, even into college, was also difficult. She shied away from that as much as she could, but when not given another choice, she found stringing thoughts together in a short amount of time and articulating them aloud were not things she was cut out for. It also did not help when others would rush her through..

Quiet was what she had always been and what she decided was easiest to stick to.

...

As shame and embarrassment continued internally,
anxiety and not wanting to disappoint or upset others
quickly became influencing forces. In the process, she
learned how to look and anticipate others' needs,
emotions and well-being, all ahead of her own.

She grew tired, exhausted, worn out, depleted as time
passed; feeling like she did not have anything else to
give. Her strength was wearing, both physically and
emotionally.

...

One day, she walked by a garden. One she had never
seen before, though she had gone this way many, many
times. It had a somewhat winding path with several
spirals along the way, filled with an abundance of
colorful wildflowers, dahlias, rose bushes, low-growing
piggyback plants, wheatgrass, a small scatter of
eucalyptus, weeping willow and Linden trees, and a little
wishing well towards the center with lily pads and lotus
flowers permeating the surface. A handful of frogs sat
afloat, croaking out a song.

As she went to sit on a jade colored bench amidst the
peach rose bushes, a vision came to her. A silhouette of

the right side of a bearded man from the chest up, with his right hand held out. Within this hand was a clear glass globe. Within that globe was her, sitting on that very bench. The man was gazing very gently, fondly at her.

Her breath caught.

"God?" she barely managed to whisper. ..

2. "Could It Be?"

As the days passed, she continued to go back to that garden every day, seeking some kind of sign, truth, knowledge, answer that her heart and soul had been yearning for for so long.

"Could it be...? .." she wondered...

For fear of causing any suspicion or drama, she went as much in secret as she could.

Each time, there was something that would have been so subtle for her to catch before, but for some reason, now it caught her eye. The shimmering on a piece of the spiderweb in the sunlight. The way the clouds wisped and bent a certain way according to the wind. The fallen leaves, dancing, twirling, high and low, in the breeze. The way the tree branches crafted into a wonderous canopy and, if she stood in the exact spot, could see and feel the sun pouring through all at once onto her.

But most of all, the rosebuds. Especially the one that was so closed up, yet had distinct hints of the deepest, most vibrant of colors around the outer petals and within.

"...God, is that truly You?" she asked out loud, into the
abyss.

Just then a whole mass of birds flew up into the sky in a
flock. It caught her breath. .. And she knew.

From that moment on, something in her heart felt as
though it was soaring up there with them every time she
saw a flock fly up together. ... How she longed to be up
there, and stay up with them...

3. The Burnt-In Leaves

She began questioning herself, who she was, what place she had in society and in the whole grand scheme of things.

Everything she had known and had learned or been made to care about — education, success, finding the love of her life, money; how socially apt she could be and appeared, how nicely but not too much nor too showy she dressed and looked, what she was going to do with her college degree, if she was worried since she hadn't gotten any calls back on job offers post-graduation, the fact she hadn't found anyone to be with ever — did they really, actually matter...?

Her love of music, singing and writing remained.

...

One day she found the beginning of a new tree in the garden, by the jade colored bench along the peach rose bushes. It had not been there before that she could recall. What stood out about it was this kind of golden glow on and around it. She was curious but uncertain..

Then she heard her name boom out from within it:

"LEA!"

... "..God...?" she answered, eyes wide open, awakened..

"Take this leaf."

The tree grew a leaf right then, and on it had the words burned in, "I am the Truth, the Way, and the Life. Whoever believes in Me will have life everlasting."

She gasped and immediately got on her knees, bowing her head down deeply... certain in the answer this time ..

"How do I move forward with this new knowledge?"

Another leaf grew, and on it, burned in again, was
written:

"Go therefore and make disciples of all nations, baptizing
them in the name of the Father and of the Son and of the
Holy Spirit (Mat 28:19)."

"...Where do I even begin, Lord...?"

He spoke this time.

"Start small, right where you are. Whether in your home,
work, community. The love, light, peace, joy and grace
you have felt are all gifts from above, meant to be
continually gifted further, wherever you find in your
Holy Spirit-compassed heart a need for Me to minister
in.

In the world you will have trouble, but remember, it is I who goes before you. I am with you. I will never abandon your side. Do not fear or be dismayed (Joh 16:33, Deu 31:8).

Trust in Me with all your heart and lean not on your own understanding; in all your ways submit to Me, and I will make your paths straight (Pro 3:5-6)."

".. Okay, Lord. .. I trust You," she replied.

The tree began sprouting more leaves in one long vine, still glowing in a golden light. Each one held new words burned in. She was so enamored by this that she gently took the whole vine and strung it around her neck.

"So I don't forget," she stated reassuringly.

And she felt the warmth of God's face shining down on
her.

4. Every Tear

Our hearts are weeping,
bleeding,
desperate for something to catch it;
hold, carry and embrace it.
While our minds logically beg to differ:
out of protection,
fear of being hurt,
made fun of,
sounding unintelligent,
cast out,
abandoned. ..

Every tear is caught
Saved
Remembered
Prayed over.
Weaved into the very tapestry that makes you You.
Used to put remnants of clay back together.

The Hands of the Potter, molding.

Until it is made anew.

5. A Love Unspoken

There was this human
The way he gazed at the other
It was telling of what was in his heart for her
The only thing was she was already married
Bound by God's love

She was drawn in yet taken aback
By the fullness, fondness and admiration she felt
Uncertain of what to do with this knowledge, awareness
It caught in her throat

Her heart cared for him
It bled for and marveled at the honesty and vulnerability
in his expression
Knowing full well he would not receive anything in
return..

Yet, he still chose to love her. ..
An unspeakable, holy kind of love
One that has not gone unnoticed

6. Single Mother By Day

There was a woman
A single mother by day
Who drew to Jesus as best she could
In being in relationship with and parenting her young
daughter

However, when struggles with transitions between one place to another, or with constant, multi-houred resistance in diaper changes ensued, it became an overwhelming battle for her.

She had made the choice of learning all she could and responding from gentle, responsive, securely attached parenting ways from the day she learned she was pregnant. Opposed to the approach her own parents had made in bringing her up. Authoritative, forceful, sometimes punishing.

When these power struggle battles took place with her daughter, something happened inside her. As if another battle took place. Conflicting feelings and thoughts — of wanting to hold space for her daughter and gently let her come to on her own; of wanting to stand her ground, make known she was the parent; and when things got to

their worst — the resistance was so strong from her
daughter and the patience had depleted from herself —
thoughts of wanting to discipline the way she had been
growing up arose. The voice of her parents telling her
she was bad in their native tongue popped into her
head.

.

.

(A reminder that, no matter how much we work and
learn to parent, guide or anything else another way, the
effects of the initial way we were treated/mistreated, if
not made aware, processed and healed, will remain in
our body's memory. The ways the mistreatment made us
feel and have to shrink ourselves will then resurface
when similar conditions occur.)

.

.

Her daughter began crying, and she saw herself as a
child in her daughter then, left emotionally unsupported.
Unseen. Fearful. She realized what a mistake she had
done and began to weep.

Somehow, with grace beyond her years, her daughter
must have felt a change in her mom, for she came over
and gave her a long embrace. Her mom took her face
into her hands and told her, "Thank you, my child, for
such generosity in your forgiveness to me."

...

"I do not set aside the grace of God, for if righteousness could be gained through the law, Christ died for nothing (Galatians 2:21)!"

Discipline, causing others, especially youngins, to obey to our commands, even out of well-meaninged intentions, is still trying to force the hand of righteousness in our own name.

In that, we have forgotten grace. That of God's, in our hearts and minds. We "set (it) aside," and in doing so, forgot how to live and be Christ-like in that moment.
...

God, help us to pause, pray and wait on You for guidance and wisdom, that stems out of Your compassion, kindness, goodwill and grace, in any given moment.

7. Let Me Have It All

"Let Me have it all, and you can rest now. For my yoke is easy and my burden is light (Matthew 11:30)."

.

.

I was just made aware, all of my unconscious tendencies and thought processing...

In this day and age of grappling, striving, trying to find and tie up any and every loose end down to the minutest of detail, attempting to perfect simply existing and being;

To convince others, and maybe even more so myself, that:

• I was a good enough person, good enough daughter, and my parents were still proud of and loved me, even during the times I got spanked

• I don't have to act perfectly, get everything "right" down to the last detail, in order to be loved and be lovable, and not be punished or shamed for it, or punish or shame myself for that matter

In this time of trying to be all that I never got or was given growing up, healing my past undealt-with trauma, and being as emotionally conscious as possible

God is telling me,

"There was never meant to be such psychological warfare within your brain, within your body. No wonder there has been such darkness and torment inside. Now that you have been made aware these things, you can let it go, give them to Me now.

Please. I can and will take care of them for you. I have already paid the price for them and made a way through.

Your task is just to lean on Me and *rest*."

8. Tale of Another Woman

There was yet another woman.

A past incident had left her combatting her own mind, marring her mental health and any sense of connection to the God she had come to know and believe in.

She went on medication to "manage" (but in truth, more keep at bay and somewhat quiet out) the ongoing intrusive thoughts running inside her head while a bout of darkness and fog quickly came over her body and mind. .. She felt she had lost herself. .. She felt lost *inside* herself...

But it was music that saved her.

Even in the most insomniatic nights where dark spiritual voices would hold her hostage in her mind in the bedroom. "Halo" (the version by Ane Brun and Linnea Olssen) played on repeat through the night out by the couch where she moved to temporarily, and was the only thing that made her feel an inkling close to God, kept the voices away, grounded her and made her feel safe enough to fall asleep.

Being in therapy was also a saving grace. It uncovered so much of her past, remaining wounds, unspoken desires and needs of her heart. Along with journeying with God as faithfully as she could, therapy aided in carving a path for her back to herself and rediscovering her voice and sense of meaning in life and living.

Believing who God says she is:

A child of God.

Daughter of the King.

Innocent.

Loved.

Pure.

Sanctified.

Intrusive thoughts not defining her worth, value or who she is. Feeling into and sharing the Love, Grace, Compassion, and Peace she had been gifted and continues to hold onto dearly.

And now, several years later, music continues to speak

and minister the most to her heart, and reconciles her
back, and closer, to God every time, along with to all of
her beloved brothers and sisters in Christ.

9. Time Has No Relevance in Eternity

I walk up to the keyboard rather hesitantly in front of my peers to stand by the choir director. When I get up there, everything disappears, becomes the space within the room. All I can really sense and see are the director, keyboard, music sheets and the awareness of myself being there.

It wasn't black in the room, but I don't know how to describe it.. It wasn't super brightly lit nor was it super dim either.. It was neutral, with some hints of light with orangey-reddish brown energy-wavelength outlines/edges and, at times, a little burst of white light.

As the director began playing the song on the keyboard, and I, singing, .. it was like there wasn't time.. or time kind of stood still, yet the present continued going, just being .. There was no pressing or pushing for anything. Everything was in harmony, at ease. There was just the present that continued to be present.. It was peaceful, calm, restful, content with itself.. Quietly enigmatic. ..

I quickly realized, time has no relevance in the timeframe of Eternity. .. I would have been fully content staying there, heart solely set on music and worshipping, praising Jesus, our Lord and Savior, for the rest of my life if I had been given the option to.

10. Anxiety / Perfect Trust

A small, blood-red colored book titled "Perfect Trust" by Charles R. Swindoll (which I spontaneously came upon in a thrift store, looked passed for a moment, felt compelled to pick up and, when I looked back to find, had the hardest time of relocating it. Had to rescan with eyes squinted at least three times back and forth before spotting it again) laid on my heart something crucial about having worry and anxiety that I hadn't recognized before.

To have either or both means to be "distracted" and have our attention "divided" from the comforting presence of God in that moment. It keeps us from being able to discern clearly what He wills for us and prevents us from allowing what *He* is capable of doing, in all of its capacity and spiritual strength, in any given moment or situation.

If I am too busy and feeling hurried, trying to make sure everything on the needs-done list is accomplished with all the quality effort I have, within a particular timeframe, at what point do I have time to commune with God and search for His wisdom and guidance? I tend not to then. It is typically me against myself in

these situations and is something I am working on fully
surrendering to Him.

...

God did not intend for us to have every single detail
figured out to be deemed the most or best of anything.
Whether that be the most/best caring parent, successful
or accomplished (_insert occupation_), etc. Actually
those are not for us to figure out at all, but rather to fall
into His guidance, direction and will.

"You will keep in perfect peace those whose minds are
stayed on You, because they trust in You (Isaiah 26:3)."

To trust Him and accept what we are being dealt at any
given moment. Completely. Even, and especially, when it
is the most difficult, unwieldy, darkest, uncertain, trivial
of times. (I am reaffirming this to myself as this is being
written.)

We are not meant to have every detailed figured out,
because God already does. And when we give it to Him
completely — boy, how powerfully transcendent and
miraculous He can make of something so chaotic and
broken.

...

Thank You, God, for providing for our every need at the right time — Your time — and guiding me in my struggle with letting go of having it all prepared and ready, as a mom and, I am quickly finding, every other facet of my life.

Without our struggles and our very humanness, we would not have a need for You and Your Grace, upon ourselves and one another.

But *that's the thing* — we **do** need You.

11. The Surgeon

I won't soon forget what took place this past Easter.

I was in deep prayer, struggling with a specific situation and set of circumstances I could not control. At one point, I vividly remember everything around me disappeared from my physical sight, and I felt the Holy Spirit wanting to search for something in my heart space. I was resistant the first two times, mentally and internally blocking It/Him from entering. I could feel Him gently nudging me, that this was important and needed, for my own self. ..I finally breathed and relented.

I felt It/Him move through my upper left chest area towards my heart. When It/He got there, I could feel Him searching. Moments later I saw, internally, and physically (somehow) felt that He found this deep jagged, long, semi-crooked crack/line by my heart, and I just remember feeling actual pain and moaning out loud, "Ow..."

Then He was working on it. I could feel that, too. He worked on it as though He was mending it. I knew He was done with it when that entire crack/line blended back into the rest of the area in my heart space, which was kind of a blur of reddish-gray-black.

At that moment, there was this huge release of a momentous pain; one that I had not known was there. I just remember feeling like everything was set back to being right again in my heart.. not actually knowing how I knew it was *"right,"* but just knowing that it was...

12. You Came In

I don't want to feel like this forever
But it's been so long since I've seen or felt
The warmth of the sun, over me
And I've been held down so long

The clouds in my mind
They keep me trailing behind
Fearing my voice and thoughts
Leaving me wondering, confused with myself

But then You came in
You showed me what Love could be
You lifted me up past, beyond those clouds
That lingering fog...
And now I can see
My mind is finally free!

I can breathe again ♡

13. "How Much More?"

I keep wondering, and know it can be rather self-focused, petty and not pretty, but I do feel this way at times, especially when tensions, struggles, hardships, stress and overwhelm are climactic: "How much more?! How much more do I have to endure? ... I don't know how much more I can handle..."

I hope (and want to believe) that I'm not the only one, if we're being honest.

This morning several things weren't going as usual. Even trying to find my way to the bathroom right across from the bedroom at 4am in the dark, and on the way, somehow clamping my thumb between the inner side of the door and the doorway as I attempted to close the door behind me. I might have muttered several things under my breath that I shan't share here, trying to deal with the pain as quietly as I could, to keep from waking anyone else up.

While sitting in the restroom after, mulling things over and wondering how and what of different natures — in the middle of this mental chaos — a voice spoke quietly but clearly to me, saying, "I love you."

And I just started bawling..

Because what those three words meant to me right in that moment was:

"I love you in all your imperfection. ♥ I love you **because of your humanness.** That is *what draws Me closer to you,* you closer to Me. I love you because I created you, long before you were in your mother's womb, in My Image, of Perfect Love. I know everything there is to know about you, even if you haven't discovered it yet (hint: you will ;)

And guess what? There is nothing, *no thing* that will ever make Me love you any less or withhold grace from you. (I apologize others have done that to you.. that is conditional loving.)

.

.

I know you are suffering.. Please know, I see it and I see you, and I am right here with you. Enduring in the pain and heartache with you. You are not alone. .. I have

already made a way through. Please, stay longer with it.
For Love's sake.

Abide in Me. I will keep you comforted, your mind at
peace, your heart in safety, under My wings. You are
protected, and so treasured and precious to Me."

——

It is no longer about suffering that I have gone through
or am currently going through, but about enduring for
and in The Name of Jesus.

His Love overcoming.

14. "Is She Going to Be Okay?"

Is it possible to be so fully attuned to the Holy Spirit and emotionally conscious that one can actually feel the immensity of the pain and suffering that another is going through in real time?

I felt the crippling anguish of hers, without realizing it was her at first. Until You made me aware.

I was so scared for her..

"Is she going to be okay?"

I could barely breathe.. waiting for the answer... *if.. when* You would answer...

And then I felt You *catch* and take hold of my heart, immediately putting it to rest as You said, *"Yes, she is."*

Trustingly I nodded, an immense amount of relief falling over my shoulders.

.

.

.

Thank You, Abba Father, for your capacity to heal us back to whole ♡

15. Together

Maybe we have been misguided
To think that self-independence and reliance are the key

I've been on that road
And boy, is it lonely
Especially when I'm deep in the middle of a struggle

Who do I go to?
Where do I turn?
Is there anyone I can trust to be there for me....?
Hurt and let down so many times...
Who do I turn to?

But You showed me it is okay to let my guard down
Little by little
To trust and open up my heart again
Even if it hurts, I know now that it has been worth it
To be on the receiving end of a love that is unbreakable,
unrelenting
Won't shift at any uncertainty, mistake, fear, hurt or
blame...
Is **Indefinite**

It's something worth sharing

And we'll carry it together
No matter what comes our way
The Strength and Determination
Willpower
Perseverance
of several can outlast that of one

So we'll keep bearing forward
Trusting that God has a plan
Darkness to Light
Like He's always been able to
Only the way that He can

16. You and I

You and I. Our lives collided for a reason. God knew we needed each other in a unique way.

Thank you for your friendship. For being, and choosing to stay, in my life ♡

17. Tangible

God is so so tangible. He is making Himself known and felt in all kinds of ways throughout each day. ..I just need to fully, completely give way to the Holy Spirit to attune me — my ears, eyes, heart, mind, soul — in seeing, feeling, experiencing, interacting, being. ..

Without Him, I am nothing.

Without Him, without acknowledging and thanking Him, the gifts He has blessed me with reap/sow nothing.

Without Him, my heart and mind become tarnished.

Without Him, I wouldn't know grace or a love that is forever unchanging, have experienced them or be able to extend them to others.

Without Him, I would still be lost. Even more wandering than I already had been. ..

With Him though — that has changed *everything*.

.

.

♬ "I called, You answered. And You came to my rescue,
and I - I want to be where You are. .."
(Came to My Rescue - Hillsong UNITED)

18. On The Cross

This is Jesus on the Cross.

He was so in tune with every other person's, each of our:
- heartaches,
- pains,
- regrets,
- fears,
- doubts,
- worries,
- meltdowns,
- darkness,
- struggles,
- anger,
- injustices,
- disappointments,
- despair,
- hatred,
- breaking points,

that He took them *fully on as His own* as He bled out.

- Through the nails hammered into His open palms and feet
- The thorn of crowns (symbolizing the consequence of sin (Gen 3:17-18)) wedged into His head that He was

made to wear out of mockery by Roman soldiers (Mat 27:27-29)

- The piercing in His side by spear later on after He had already died (John 19:33-34)

Not only was He willingly and acceptingly taking it all on as His own, for God's will and eternal glory, He remained compassionate and grace-filled in heart, even forgiving the two men (thieves) crucified on either side of Him who were also mocking and insulting Him (Isaiah 53:12).

"*Father, forgive them, for they know not what they do* (Luke 23:34)," He pleaded on their behalf.

As Jesus continued to pray out to God through his suffering, one thief gradually had a change in heart, rebuking the other for continuing to insult Jesus, saying, "Do you not fear God, since you are under the same sentence of condemnation? And we indeed justly, for we are receiving the due reward of our deeds; but this man has done nothing wrong (Luke 23:39–41)."

He was defending Jesus, now believing He was and is the King, the Savior He had claimed to be all along.

His next words were a plea:

"Jesus, remember me when you come into your Kingdom (Luke 23:42)."

And Jesus responded with all the love and compassion He had already had for this man:

"Truly, I say to you, today you will be with me in paradise (Luke 23:43)."

It is never too late to come to/come back to Jesus, to God. He has loved you all along and always cares for you, no matter the distance you ever (illusively) create between Him and yourself.

God's gift of salvation and grace are never something you have to earn. They are something received simply through belief and faith, knowing within there is a dire need for them.

19. Music / When We Sing

Music
Could it be a gateway into Heaven?
Ageless
Timeless

When we sing
In harmony
All I see is this orange and white glow
Breaking through the darkness
Opening up the skies
Swooping down and wide
Wrapping all around us

It washes everything away
When I find You within the song
The melody
So tenderly..
It is gently overcoming
Blanketed in abundance
By Your Light, Awestruck Wonder, Presence and Love ..

How You love us so ♡

20. In My Heart

Eyes open
Heart racing
The noise, chaos around me erupt in my head
Affecting the ability to think, see and hear straight
Searching for my voice
But it is stuck somewhere way down in my throat

I close my eyes
Press and breathe into my heart space
As I do, I am met by the Holy Spirit
Who slows it down
Calms it
Holds and carries it
Causes it to beat deeply and rhythmicly in my chest that
I can feel, and even hear it if I stay quietly tuned
inward...
Recovers it

"Don't worry, Momma.
It's always okay,"
I hear my daughter say ❤

...

I know I am safe

I have been found
And can find Jesus at any moment while I'm on this
earth
— In my heart.
Until He calls me home